Introduction to 🌍 EARTH'S RESOURCES

HOW WE USE
WOOD

Nancy Dickmann

Crabtree Publishing Company
www.crabtreebooks.com

Crabtree Publishing Company
www.crabtreebooks.com

Author: Nancy Dickmann
Editorial Director: Kathy Middleton
Editor: Ellen Rodger
Picture Manager: Sophie Mortimer
Design Manager: Keith Davis
Children's Publisher: Anne O'Daly
Proofreader: Debbie Greenberg
Production coordinator and Prepress technician: Ken Wright
Print coordinator: Katherine Berti

Photographs (t=top, b=bottom, l=left, r=right, c=center)
Front Cover: All images Shutterstock
Interior: iStock: catalby 1, George Clerk 20, DmitryPK 13, DuxX 21, fabphoto 27, Ijubaphoto 15, IwonaWawroo 4, Joroivo 5, Kamisokai 24, KatePhotographer 23, luoman 22, Monkey Business Images 14, morenosoppeisa 19, olm26250 18, SafakOfuz 11, StockStudiox 10, Steve Stone 25, Gill Tukha 26, Mrs Vega 16, zingmin 6; Shutterstock: Bartosz Nitkiewicz 17, Petro Perutskyi 29br, Photographee.eu 28t, singkham 28b, stock 7, 12, Patricia Peceguini Viana 9, welcomia 8, Yeti Studio 29cl.
All facts, statistics, web addresses and URLs in this book were verified as valid and accurate at time of writing. No responsibility for any changes to external websites or references can be accepted by either the author or publisher.

Library and Achives Canada Cataloguing in Publication

Title: How we use wood / Nancy Dickmann.
Names: Dickmann, Nancy, author.
Description: Series statement: Introduction to Earth's resources | Includes bibliographical references and index.
Identifiers: Canadiana (print) 20200284541 | Canadiana (ebook) 20200284576 | ISBN 9780778781998 (softcover) | ISBN 9780778781851 (hardcover) | ISBN 9781427126030 (HTML)
Subjects: LCSH: Wood—Utilization—Juvenile literature. | LCSH: Wood—Juvenile literature.
Classification: LCC SD541 .D53 2020 | DDC j620.1/2—dc23

Library of Congress Cataloging-in-Publication Data

Names: Dickmann, Nancy, author.
Title: How we use wood / Nancy Dickmann.
Description: New York, NY : Crabtree Publishing Company, 2021. | Series: Introduction to earth's resources | Includes index.
Identifiers: LCCN 2020029715 (print) | LCCN 2020029716 (ebook) | ISBN 9780778781851 (hardcover) | ISBN 9780778781998 (paperback) | ISBN 9781427126030 (ebook)
Subjects: LCSH: Wood--Utilization--Juvenile literature.
Classification: LCC SD541 .D53 2021 (print) | LCC SD541 (ebook) | DDC 620.1/2--dc23
LC record available at https://lccn.loc.gov/2020029715
LC ebook record available at https://lccn.loc.gov/2020029716

Crabtree Publishing Company
www.crabtreebooks.com   1-800-387-7650
Published in 2021 by Crabtree Publishing Company
Copyright © Brown Bear Books Ltd 2020

Published in Canada
Crabtree Publishing
616 Welland Ave.
St. Catharines, ON
L2M 5V6

Published in the United States
Crabtree Publishing
347 Fifth Ave
Suite 1402-145
New York, NY 10016

Printed in the U.S.A./082020/CG20200710

In Canada: We acknowledge the financial support of the Government of Canada through the Canada Book Fund for our publishing activities.

Contents

What Is Wood?

It grows all over Earth and we use it every day. What is it? It's wood, of course!

Wood is the hard, sturdy part of trees and some other types of plants. When the plant is alive, wood is part of the system that sends water and minerals from its roots to its other parts. Once the tree is cut down, people use the wood.

The trunk and branches of a tree are made of wood.

About 3,000–4,000 different species of plants produce wood we can use.

Throughout history, many homes have been built from wood.

Using Wood

Wood is a very useful material. Humans have been using it for hundreds of thousands of years. It can be burned as a **fuel**, carved into shapes, or made into paper. Wood is strong but fairly light, and it is easy to work with.

Scientists have found evidence that humans were carving wood 1.5 million years ago.

Where Wood Comes From

Wood comes from trees. These amazing plants grow on all continents except for Antarctica.

Trees need air, water, and sunlight to grow. They cannot grow in places where it is too cold or there is not enough water. There are few trees in deserts, and none in the **polar regions**. But thick forests grow in many other places around the world.

The dark green areas on this map show forests.

There are more than **16 million square miles** (2.6 million square km) of forests in the world.

This means that nearly **31%** of the world's land is covered in forests.

This seedling will one day grow into a huge oak tree.

From Seed to Tree

A tree starts as a simple seed, such as an acorn. Once it takes root in the ground, it will begin to grow upward. Branches covered in leaves will spread out. It can take many years for a tree to reach its full height. After that, its trunk will still continue to grow thicker.

Types of Wood

There are many different types of trees. That means there are many different types of wood, too!

Most wood is a shade of brown—anything from pale tan to a deep chocolate color. However, some trees produce wood that is reddish, pinkish, or even an olive green color. When you cut into wood, it shows a pattern called a **grain**. Each type of wood has its own grain.

The wood of a giant sequoia tree is a dark reddish brown.

Wood absorbs water. Water often makes up **8–25%** of the weight of a piece of wood.

A balsa tree produces a type of hardwood that is very lightweight and soft.

Hard or Soft?

Wood that comes from a tree with cones and needles, such as a pine tree, is called softwood. Wood that comes from a tree that loses its leaves in winter, such as an oak or a maple tree, is called hardwood. But these are just names. Some types of hardwood are actually soft, and some types of softwood are fairly hard!

The hardest wood comes from the Guaiacum tree, or holywood. It is **three times** harder than oak.

Logging

We cut down trees to use their wood. This is called logging. It is one of the world's biggest industries.

When a farmer picks apples, the apple tree survives. It will produce more apples next year. But we must cut a whole tree down to use its wood. A new tree can be planted to replace it. Some trees are ready to cut in just a few years. Other types must grow for 100 years or more before they are ready.

People who work in logging are traditionally known as lumberjacks.

Cutting and Preparing

Loggers often use **chainsaws** to cut down trees. Once the tree is down, they cut off the large branches. The bark is removed and the trunk is cut into logs. The logs are taken to a **sawmill** on trucks. There, they can be sawn into planks or chopped into wood chips.

More than **200 million tons** (181 million metric tons) of sawn wood are produced each year.

About **20%** of this sawn wood comes from Russia.

Building with Wood

Wood has always been a popular material for building homes.

Early people used stone tools to cut and shape wood. They built simple homes, often covered with a roof made of straw or other plant material. Hundreds of years ago, strong wooden beams began to be used to make the **frame** of a house. The walls were filled in with materials such as mud, clay, or bricks.

The Vikings built large longhouses out of wood.

Archaeologists have found the remains of a wooden house built **10,000 years** ago.

Wooden Homes Today

Many homes are still built with wooden frames. Wood is also sawn into thin planks or panels and used as an outer covering on the frame. Frames made from steel beams are also common. Tall modern skyscrapers are built with steel beams not wood.

About 93% of new homes built in the United States have a wooden frame.

A wooden frame is cheap and quick to put together.

Wood in the Home

Wood can do much more than build a strong frame. It is used throughout many homes!

If you look around, you'll see wood in most rooms of a house. Many homes have wooden floorboards. Furniture is often made from wood. There is wood in picture frames and many window frames. In kitchens you'll find cutting boards and utensils made of wood.

Wood is one of the main materials used to make furniture.

Around the world, people spend about **$285 billion** on wooden furniture every year.

The furniture maker Ikea uses **1%** of the world's commercial wood supply.

Even sofas and armchairs often have a wooden frame beneath their soft covering.

Some skilled woodworkers still make furniture by hand.

Why Choose Wood?

Most types of wood are inexpensive and easy to shape. Wood can be sanded to a smooth finish. Applying stain or oil to the wood lets its beautiful grain show. These **properties** make it perfect for flooring and furniture. Many people also paint the wood in their home in a range of different colors.

Wood as Fuel

One of the earliest ways that humans used wood was by burning it as a fuel.

As long as it is dry, wood burns well and produces heat and light. It is easily available, so for thousands of years, it was the most common fuel for cooking and heating. In many parts of the world, people still rely on it. Others enjoy the cozy warmth of a wood fire in their fireplace.

The light and heat of a campfire make camping trips fun.

Wood provides about **6%** of energy around the world.

The smoke from a wood fire gives a special flavor to meat, fish, and cheese.

Wood Today

Instead of logs, many people burn small pellets. They are made of sawdust and other products made from leftover wood. Pellets can fuel a wood stove, but they can also be burned to produce **electricity** at a power plant. Unfortunately, burning wood causes air **pollution**.

3.5 million households in the United States use wood as their main heating fuel.

Paper

There is one wood product that you probably use every day: paper.

Paper was first invented about 2,000 years ago. Since then, it has become one of the most useful products we make. There is paper everywhere in modern life, from books and newspapers to toilet paper and cereal boxes. Paper bags carry goods we buy at the store, and online orders are shipped in cardboard boxes.

A layer of wavy paper sandwiched between two flat pieces makes strong cardboard.

 More than **460 million tons** (417 million metric tons) of paper and cardboard are produced each year.

 At least **50%** of paper and cardboard is used for packaging.

Making Paper

Most paper is made from fast-growing trees such as pine. The wood is chopped into chips, then mashed into a pulp. This releases the natural fibers in the wood. Adding chemicals makes the fibers white and strong. The wet pulp is spread out and pressed to form flat sheets, which are then dried.

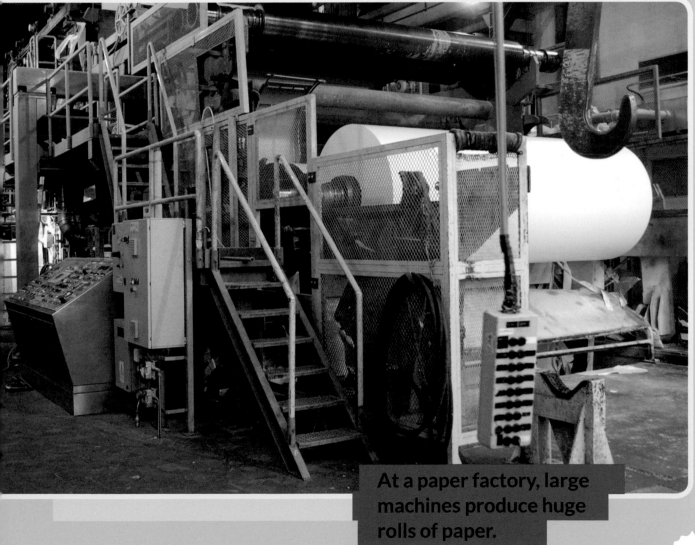

At a paper factory, large machines produce huge rolls of paper.

Is Wood Renewable?

Wood is one of the world's most important resources. We use huge amounts of it every day.

Some resources, such as oil, are not **renewable**. There is only a limited amount of them on Earth. Once we have used that up, there will be no more. Wood is different. It is a renewable resource. If a tree is cut down to be made into furniture or paper, a new one can grow to replace it.

One day, these saplings will form a towering pine forest.

Since humans first began cutting down trees, tree numbers have gone down by about **46%**.

Without replanting the trees we cut down, forests could disappear.

Planting More

Wood is only truly renewable if we plant trees to replace the ones that we cut down. This does not always happen. Long ago, there were many more trees than there are now. Today, logging companies can earn a certificate to show that they are managing forests well by replacing trees and keeping them healthy.

Scientists estimate that about **15 billion** trees are cut down each year.

Deforestation

Sometimes loggers cut down large areas of forest. This is called deforestation.

People cut down many trees so that they can use the wood. But there are other reasons for **deforestation**, too. Farmers may want to clear land to grow **crops** or raise **livestock**. Miners clear trees before drilling or digging into the ground. People may want the land for building roads, factories, or homes.

Around the world, people are planting fewer trees than they cut down.

13,000 square miles (34,000 square km) of forest are lost each year.

In the last **50 years**, about **17%** of the Amazon **rain forest** has been cut down.

Some of the worst deforestation is taking place in the world's rain forests.

The rain forests where orangutans live are being destroyed.

Not Enough Trees

The effects of deforestation are serious. Many people, especially in poorer countries, depend on forests for fuel. There are also huge numbers of animals living in the world's forests. When forests are cut down, it destroys their **habitats**. Some animals are at risk of **extinction** because of deforestation.

The Lungs of the Planet

Trees are more than just materials for humans to use. Without trees, life on Earth would probably be impossible.

Air is made of a mix of gases, including **oxygen** and **carbon dioxide** (CO_2). Humans and animals need to breathe in oxygen. We breathe out CO_2 as a waste gas, or a gas we do not need. Trees and other plants do the opposite! They take in CO_2 and release oxygen into the air. Trees also filter the air, or keep it clean.

Leaves use energy from the Sun to turn CO_2 and water into food for the plant and oxygen.

Some scientists estimate that the world has about **3.04 trillion** trees.

That is nearly **400** trees for every human on Earth.

Climate Change

Burning fuels releases CO_2 into the **atmosphere**. The gas builds up like a blanket. It traps the Sun's heat close to Earth, like glass in a greenhouse does. This buildup is warming up Earth and causing **climate change**. The world's forests help by reduce the effect by taking a huge amount of CO_2 out of the air.

Climate change is already starting to cause more frequent floods and storms.

Forest Fires

It takes many years for a forest to grow. A fire can destroy a whole forest in days.

Wood burns well—that's why it's such a useful fuel. It also means forests can catch fire more easily. A campfire or a cigarette can start a fire. So can lightning or strong heat from the Sun. Once a fire starts, it spreads over the ground and moves from tree to tree.

Large forest fires can create winds that help spread the fire.

A forest fire can spread at up to **14 miles per hour** (22.5 km/h).

Firefighting airplanes drop water or foam on forest fires.

Fire Danger

The drier the trees the faster the fire can spread. The fires that started in 2019 in Australia were made much worse by dry conditions. Big forest fires are difficult to fight. They can destroy homes and anything else in their path. They also kill huge numbers of forest animals.

Scientists estimate that more than **1 billion** animals died in the Australian forest fires that raged in 2019–2020.

What Can I Do?

Wood is a precious resource. Here are some tips on how you can protect it.

- Don't waste paper! You can use the back of a piece of paper for doodling or making notes.

- Recycle used paper and cardboard packaging.

- Look for products that are made from recycled paper, such as notebooks or toilet paper.

- When buying products made from wood or paper, look for the **FSC** logo. It shows that the wood came from a forest that is managed well.

- If you have space in your garden, plant a tree or two!

Quiz

How much have you learned about wood? It's time to test your knowledge!

1. What three things do trees need to grow?

a. oxygen, sugar, and sap

b. moonlight, sparkles, and hugs

c. air, water, and sunlight

2. What is the pattern in wood called?

a. grain

b. strain

c. brain

3. Which gas do trees release into the air?

a. oxygen

b. carbon dioxide

c. helium

4. Why is wood a renewable resource?

a. it doesn't cause pollution

b. we can plant new trees to replace the ones we cut down

c. it can be made into lots of different products

5. What kind of tools did early humans use to cut and shape wood?

a. chainsaws

b. stone tools

c. Swiss Army knives

Answers on page 32.

Glossary

atmosphere The blanket of gases that surrounds Earth

carbon dioxide A gas found naturally in the atmosphere, which is also produced when we burn fuels

chainsaws Mechanical tools with teeth on a moving chain

climate change The change in Earth's climate as a result of human actions

crops Plants that are grown for food

deforestation Clearing a wide area of trees without replacing them

electricity The flow of current that we use to run gadgets, motors, lights, and more

extinction The state of dying out completely as a species

frame A sturdy structure that supports a building

FSC Short form for Forest Stewardship Council

fuel A substance that is burned to release energy

grain The pattern of fibers in wood

habitats The natural homes of animals or plants

livestock Animals, such as cattle, raised on farms for food

oxygen A gas found in the atmosphere, which plants produce and humans need to survive

polar regions The very cold areas near Earth's North and South Poles

pollution The dirtying of water, air, or other environments by harmful substances

properties Characteristics of a material, such as color or hardness

rain forest An area of dense forest that receives a lot of rain

renewable Able to be replaced rather than being used up entirely

sawmill A building with machinery for sawing or making wood products

Find out More

Books

Ryckman, Tatiana. *How is Paper Made and Sold?* (Where Do Goods Come From?). Cavendish Square, 2019.

Silen, Andrea. *Rainforests* (National Geographic Readers). National Geographic Children's Books, 2020.

Socha, Piotr. *Trees: A Rooted History.* Abrams Books, 2019.

Spilsbury, Louise and Richard. *Forest Biomes* (Earth's Natural Biomes). Crabtree Publishing, 2018.

Websites

www.explainthatstuff.com/papermaking.html
This website has information about how paper is made.

www.logcabinhub.com/living-with-wood-from-the-beginning-of-time/
Visit this website to find out how wood has been used through the ages.

www.nationalgeographic.com/environment/global-warming/deforestation/
This website explains how deforestation affects wildlife, habitats, and climate change.

Index

Quiz answers

1. c; 2. a; 3. a; 4. b; 5. b